W

SO-ANN-608

3 1192 00649 9782

PICTURE LIBRARY

RACING

INTERIM SITE

PICTURE LIBRARY
RACING CARS

N. S. Barrett

Franklin Watts

London   New York   Sydney   Toronto

© 1984 Franklin Watts Ltd

First published in Great Britain
    1984 by
Franklin Watts Ltd
12a Golden Square
London W1

First published in the USA by
Franklin Watts Inc
387 Park Avenue South
New York
N.Y. 10016

First published in Australia by
Franklin Watts
1 Campbell Street
Artarmon, NSW 2064

U.S. ISBN: 0-531-15143-3 (pbk)
US ISBN: 0-531-03784-3
Library of Congress Catalog Card
Number: 84-50018

Designed by
McNab Design

Photographs by
Jeff Bloxham; Ford Motor Co Ltd;
Renault Cars Ltd; Thrust Cars Ltd;
Porsche Ltd; Leo Mason;
Don Morley; Bob Thomas

Illustrated by
Tony Bryan

Technical Consultant
Marcus Pye

Contents

Introduction

Motor racing is full of excitement. Drivers battle for the lead as they steer their racing cars round tight corners and then go full speed along the straightaways. Round and round they go, for lap after lap. Some drop out when their cars break down or crash. The winner is the driver who crosses the finishing line first.

△A Brabham-BMW Formula One car driven by World Champion Nelson Piquet of Brazil. Cars carry the names of their sponsors—the companies who provide the money to build and race them.

Many kinds of cars take part in races. They range from powerful racing machines, called "Formula One" cars, to small karts. Sports cars and sedan cars also race and there are competitions for special cars called dragsters.

△ A powerful sports car takes a bend in very wet conditions. Special grooved tires are used in the rain.

The racing car

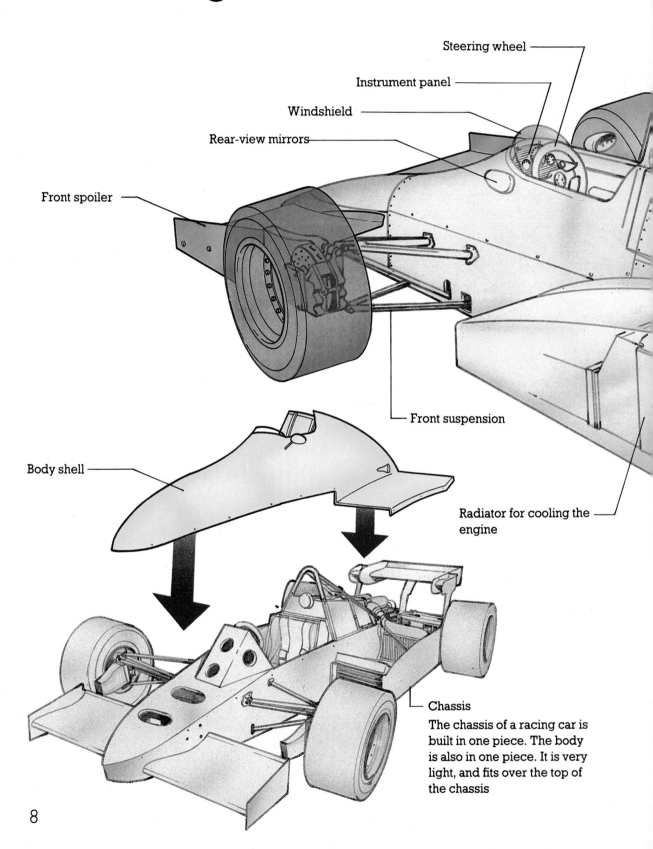

Steering wheel

Instrument panel

Windshield

Rear-view mirrors

Front spoiler

Front suspension

Body shell

Radiator for cooling the engine

Chassis
The chassis of a racing car is built in one piece. The body is also in one piece. It is very light, and fits over the top of the chassis

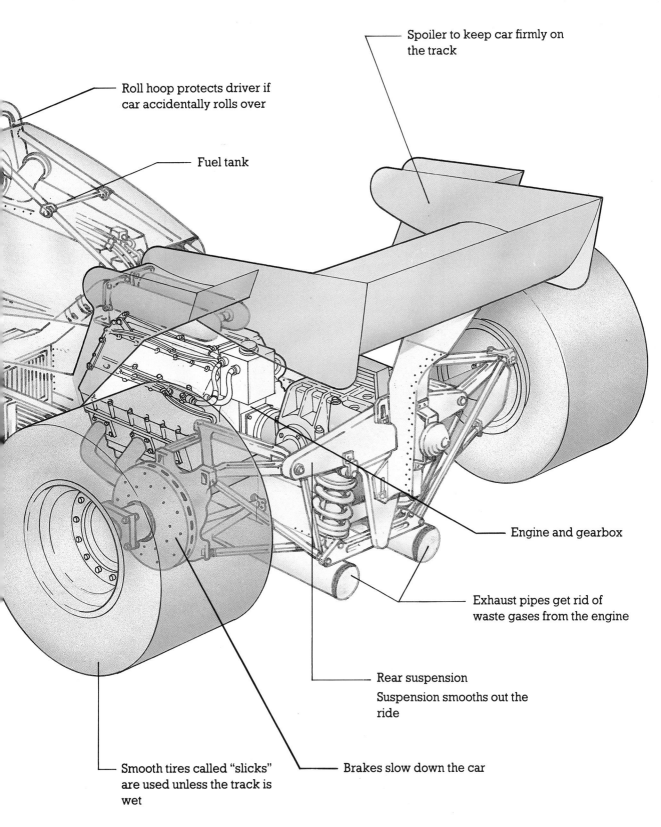

Spoiler to keep car firmly on the track

Roll hoop protects driver if car accidentally rolls over

Fuel tank

Engine and gearbox

Exhaust pipes get rid of waste gases from the engine

Rear suspension
Suspension smooths out the ride

Smooth tires called "slicks" are used unless the track is wet

Brakes slow down the car

Formula One

In motor racing, there are classes called "formulas." Formulas are sets of rules that control the power and size of cars. The top class is Formula One.

A "grand prix" is an important race. Drivers earn points for finishing in the first six (9 for 1st, then 6, 4, 3, 2, 1). The driver with the most points in the year is the World Champion.

△ A modern racing car has large smooth tires. This car is an ATS, with a BMW engine.

△French driver Patrick Tambay speeds down the straightaway in a Ferrari. Red has always been the color of the famous Italian Ferrari cars.

◁The racing driver is well protected, with safety belts and a crash helmet. All his clothing is fireproof, including the face mask. The tube leading into his helmet is attached to an oxygen bottle. He might need to use this for breathing after a crash when there is fire or smoke.

◁Mechanics work on a Formula One Renault. With the body shell off, you can see the engine and a complicated mass of wires and machinery.

Other classes

Formula One racing is for the fastest cars and the best drivers. The next classes are Formula Two and Formula Three. The cars in these classes do not have such powerful engines. Most drivers start racing in a junior class called Formula Ford 1600. These cars look like racing cars, but they have ordinary road tires and engines.

△ A Formula Ford is an ideal single-seater racing car for a beginner. Its engine is similar to those used in ordinary small family cars.

△ After Formula Ford, drivers progress to Formula Three racing (above) and then Formula Two (left).

Karts

Karts are the smallest of all the racing machines. When you sit in one, you are only about 1 in (2 cm) above the ground.

Simple karts have no gearbox and only a small engine. They are ideal for beginners to learn in and to race. More powerful karts have several gears and are fitted with bigger engines.

▽ The fastest karts are like tiny racing cars. They can reach speeds of 140 mph (225 km/h).

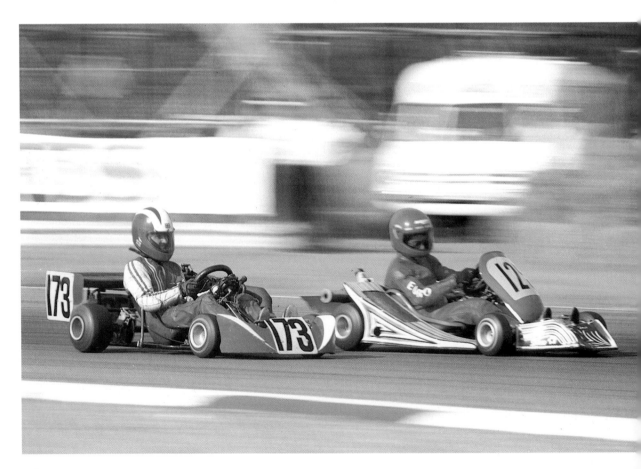

The kart was invented in 1956 by a mechanic in California. He found some spare lawn-mower engines. Using an oblong framework of steel tubing, he fixed four wheels on the corners. He then mounted an engine behind the driver's seat and fitted a steering wheel and pedals. Karting now has its own World Championships.

△ A simple kart is just a light metal frame which carries the engine and driver on tiny wheels.

Rally cars

Rallies are not really races. The rally course has several sections. Drivers must complete each section in a set time. They lose points for arriving late. Some rallies may last for a week or more.

△ A rally car takes part in the famous Monte Carlo Rally. Rally cars are often ordinary sedan cars strengthened for rough conditions. They have a driver and a navigator, who reads the map.

Dragsters

Only two cars at a time take part in drag racing. They race over a straight track called a "drag strip." It is ¼ mile (402 m) long.

There are several kinds of drag racers, or "dragsters." The fastest are called "fuellers" or "rails." These cars may reach speeds of over 250 mph (400 km/h).

▽ Powerful dragsters have a long chassis, wide back wheels and small, thin wheels in front. The race track is divided into two separate strips, one for each car. A race lasts only 5 or 6 seconds.

Off the road

Some motor sports take place off the road or ordinary racing circuits. The desert races in America and Mexico are held over very rough country. The course may be up to 1,000 miles (1,600 km) long. All kinds of cars, motorcycles and even pick-up trucks compete.

△ A "dune buggy" competing in an off-road race in the Nevada desert of the USA. Desert races really test drivers and cars. Drivers stop only for fuel or repairs.

"Rallycross" was invented in Britain in 1967. It is a race for up to 10 cars. Rallycross takes place on a special circuit with different surfaces. The course changes from tarmac to grass, chalk, and mud.

△ In rallycross, drivers need all their skills to control their cars on different surfaces. Similar sports are "autocross," raced mostly on grass, and "sand racing," on beaches.

Stock cars

Stock cars are like the ordinary sedan cars you see on the road. Those used for racing have their engines tuned for higher speeds. There are classes of stock car racing for different sizes of engines or makes of car. In Britain, it is called "saloon car" racing.

△Sedan cars race on tracks just like single-seater racing cars. They may race very close together, often touching each other.

Sports cars

A sports car is a two-seater. It often has a closed cockpit. The bodywork covers the wheels.

Famous sports car races at Le Mans, France, and Daytona, USA, go on for 24 hours. There are two or three drivers for each car. Each driver takes a turn at the wheel. While one drives round the circuit, the other can rest.

▽Sports car races can last for up to 24 hours. The most powerful sports cars are faster on most straightaways than Formula One cars.

◁Sports cars have spoilers at the back, just like Formula One cars. They have powerful headlights for driving at night in long-distance events.

The record breakers

The holder of the world land speed record is said to be the fastest person on earth. To break the record, a car must make two runs in opposite directions over either a mile or a kilometer. The car's average speed over the two runs is what counts. The car has a "flying start." That is, the driver gets up to full speed before the starting mark.

▽ British driver Richard Noble with his record-breaking car *Thrust 2*. All cars attempting the land speed record have to be specially built. *Thrust 2* has aluminum wheels because the high speeds make it too hot for rubber tires. It runs on a jet engine of the type used in some aircraft.

The contest for the land speed record began in 1898. A Frenchman drove at 39 mph (63 km/h) in an electric car. Cars running on steam and then gasoline challenged this record. In just a few years, the record was more than doubled. For the last 60 years the record has been held by either British or American cars. Rocket or jet engines are now used to give the power.

△ *Thrust 2* jets across the Black Rock Desert in Nevada in October 1983. In it, Richard Noble set a new land speed record of 633 mph (1,019 km/h). There are very few places in the world that are suitable for a record attempt. The car needs several miles of perfectly flat, dry land.

The story of racing cars

△Racing cars of over 70 years ago. A Delage chases a Lion-Peugeot in a 1911 grand prix.

The first racing cars

The motor-car was invented in the 1880s. That was when Karl Benz, a German engineer designed the first "horseless carriage." It was not long before people were racing their cars against each other. The first organized race took place on the

△Old cars are still paraded and raced. Special events are run for old machines like these.

roads of France in 1895. The winner raced at an average speed of only 15 mph (24 km/h). The winning car was a Panhard powered by a Daimler engine.

As racing became popular, manufacturers in several countries began to make faster cars. They included the Peugeot, Delage and Bugatti from France, the Fiat and Alfa Romeo from Italy, the Duesenberg from the USA, and the Bentley and Sunbeam from Britain.

Monsters

The German racing cars of the 1930s, Mercedes and Auto-Union, were "monsters" compared with those of today. Because they had big and very powerful engines, they were as fast as today's racing cars on the straightaways. But they were much slower round bends because they had narrow wheels and thin tires. The Auto-Union was the first grand prix car to have its engine mounted at the back. Now all grand prix cars have rear engines.

Italian designs

In the 1950s, the leading racing cars were designed and made in Italy. They were the Alfa Romeo, the Ferrari, and the Maserati.

Lying back

In the late 1950s, Colin Chapman, a British designer, introduced the Lotus car. Instead of sitting upright, Lotus drivers lay back, with their feet between the front wheels. Later, Lotus designs were unusual in another way. The chassis was made in one piece, from flat pieces of metal instead of tubes. Soon, all the other makes copied this one-piece, or "monocoque," design.

△ A 1983 Arrows A6. This car had a Cosworth-Ford engine.

Cosworth-Ford

For many years most Formula One cars used Cosworth-Ford DFV V8 engines. The name "Cosworth" comes from the names of its two designers, Mike COStin and Keith DuckWORTH. The engine was first used in the Lotus in 1967. But in 1968, Ford allowed other racing teams to use their engines.

△ A Renault, like most Formula One cars now, has a turbocharged engine.

Turbo engines

Nearly all Formula One racing cars now have turbocharged engines. Turbocharging is a special way of increasing an engine's power. Some of the energy that is normally wasted— as gases that come out of the exhaust pipe—is put back into the engine. The Formula One size limit on a turbocharged engine is 1½ liters instead of 3 liters for an ordinary engine.

△ The Maserati 250F was a leading make of the 1950s. They still take part in races.

Facts and records

World Champion

The World Champion is the driver who collects the most grand prix points in a year.

The driver who won most World Championships was Juan Manuel Fangio of Argentina. He won five in the 1950s.

Drag record

An American drag racer, Kitty O'Neill, set a world record in 1977. Driving a rocket-powered dragster, she covered the ¼-mile (402 m) track in 3.72 seconds. Her speed at the finish was 392 mph (632 km/h).

Grand prix winners

It is every racing driver's aim to win a grand prix. Scottish driver Jackie Stewart won 27 before he retired in 1973. Jim Clark, also a Scot, set a record by winning seven grand prix races in one year (1963).

△ Stunt drivers entertain the crowd before a big race.

Grand prix cars

Engines for grand prix cars need rebuilding after every race. This is because they stay in top condition only for about 400 miles (650 km). A grand prix race goes on for 180–250 miles (300–400 km), and there are practice laps, too.

Six-wheeler

In 1976, the British Tyrrell team designed a racing car with six wheels—two at the back as usual,

△ The Tyrrell six-wheeler.

but four at the front. People were amazed by its strange looks. But it won only one race.

Races and teams

Grand prix races take place in many countries of the world. During a motor-racing season, the racing car teams travel from country to country. A team is made up of a manager, one or more drivers and cars and several mechanics.

Glossary

cc
The letters "cc" stand for cubic centimeters. There are 1,000 cc in 1 liter. Both these units are used to measure the size of engines. See **liter** below.

Chassis
The chassis of a car is its frame, wheels and suspension. Many racing cars have a chassis built in one piece.

Formula
In motor racing, a formula is a set of rules for entering cars in a race. The rules control the size of the engine and the design of the car. Cars entering a Formula One race, for example, must be designed to follow the Formula One rules.

Liter
The size of racing car engines is measured in liters or cc. The smallest engines used in karting are 100 cc ($\frac{1}{10}$ liter). Formula One engines must not be more than 3 liters.

Monocoque
A chassis built as one piece is called a monocoque. (The word is French for "single shell.")

Roll hoop
A strong metal frame called a roll hoop is part of the car's chassis. It protects the driver from injury if the car turns over.

Slicks
Smooth tires are called "slicks." They are used only on dry circuits. In the wet, they push water in front of them and then float on it. As a result, the driver loses control.

Spoiler
The spoilers are the special pieces at the back and front of a racing car. They are designed so that the air rushing past the car pushes it down onto the track.

Tread
The pattern cut into tires is called its tread. A tire with a tread does not grip a dry, smooth surface as much as a "slick," because less of the tire is in contact with the ground. But in wet weather, the grooves allow the water to escape.

Tuning
Tuning an engine in the workshop means to put it in perfect working order.

Index